moment meditations

Prayers of the Heart

Stormie Omartian

Harvest House Publishers
Eugene, Oregon

Prayers of the Heart

Published by Harvest House Publishers
Eugene, Oregon 97402

ISBN 0-7369-0207-4

Text is adapted from *The Power of a Praying™ Wife* and *The Power of a Praying™ Parent* by Stormie Omartian (Harvest House Publishers, 1997 and 1995).

Design and production by Left Coast Design, Portland, Oregon.
Artwork by Gwendolyn Babbit

Harvest House Publishers has made every effort to trace the ownership of all poems and quotes. In the event of a question arising from the use of a poem or quote, we regret any error made and will be pleased to make the necessary correction in future editions of this book.

Printed in China.

02 03 04 05 06 07 08 / PP / 10 9 8 7 6 5 4 3

Answered prayer is a testimony to God's unfailing faithfulness. I can say without a doubt that *prayer works*! If you will lift up the concerns of your heart in prayer as the Holy Spirit leads you and look to God to be the source of all you want to see happen in your life, great things will happen. Don't worry about *how* He will answer you, just know that you can rest in Him.

Ask, and it will be given to you; seek, and you will find; knock, and it will be opened to you. For everyone who asks receives, and he who seeks finds, and to him who knocks it will be opened.

MATTHEW 7:7,8

I lift up my character to You. Take my old emotional habits, mindsets, and automatic reactions and make me patient, kind, good, faithful, gentle, and self-controlled. Please give me a new heart and work in me Your love, peace, and joy.

Daylight can be seen through very small holes, so little things will illustrate a person's character.

SAMUEL SMILES

LORD,

I pray You would bless the work of my hands. Help me to have confidence in the gifts You have placed in me to be able to seek, find, and do good work. I pray that the work You have given me would be established, secure, successful, and satisfying. Thank You for providing for me.

Let the beauty of the Lord our God be upon us, and establish the work of our hands for us; yes, establish the work of our hands.

PSALM 90:17

Work...is, or should be, the full expression of the worker's faculties, the thing in which he finds spiritual, mental, and bodily satisfaction, and the medium in which he offers himself to God.

DOROTHY L. SAYERS

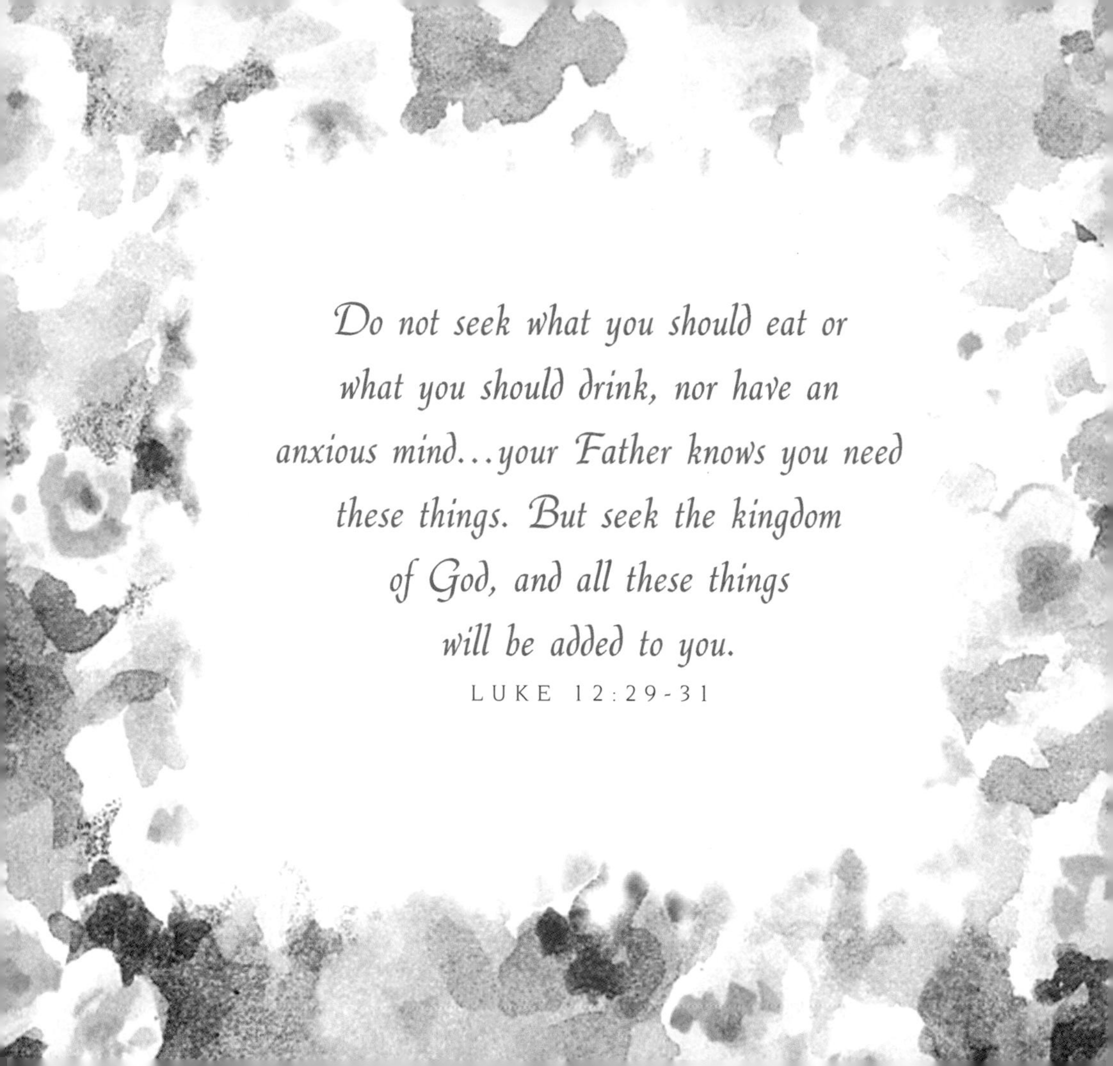

Do not seek what you should eat or what you should drink, nor have an anxious mind...your Father knows you need these things. But seek the kingdom of God, and all these things will be added to you.

LUKE 12:29-31

Lord,

I commit my finances to You. May I be a good steward of all that You have given me, and help me remember that all I have belongs to You. I pray that I will find it easy to give to You and to others. I know that if I seek Your kingdom first, all that I need will be given to me.

We make a living by what we get.
We make a life by what we give.

DUANE HULSE

I pray for an affectionate heart. Help me to demonstrate how much I care and value my family and friends. I never want to seem cold, undemonstrative, uninterested, or remote with them. Enable me instead to be warm, tender, compassionate, and caring.

Love is the leading affection of the soul.

MATTHEW HENRY

If there is any consolation in Christ,
if any comfort of love, if any fellowship of
the Spirit, if any affection and mercy, fulfill
my joy by being like-minded, having the same
love, being of one accord, of one mind.

PHILIPPIANS 2:1,2

No temptation has overtaken you except such as is common to man; but God is faithful, who will not allow you to be tempted beyond what you are able, but with the temptation will also make the way of escape; that you may be able to bear it.

1 CORINTHIANS 10:13

Temptation provokes me to look upward to God.

JOHN BUNYAN

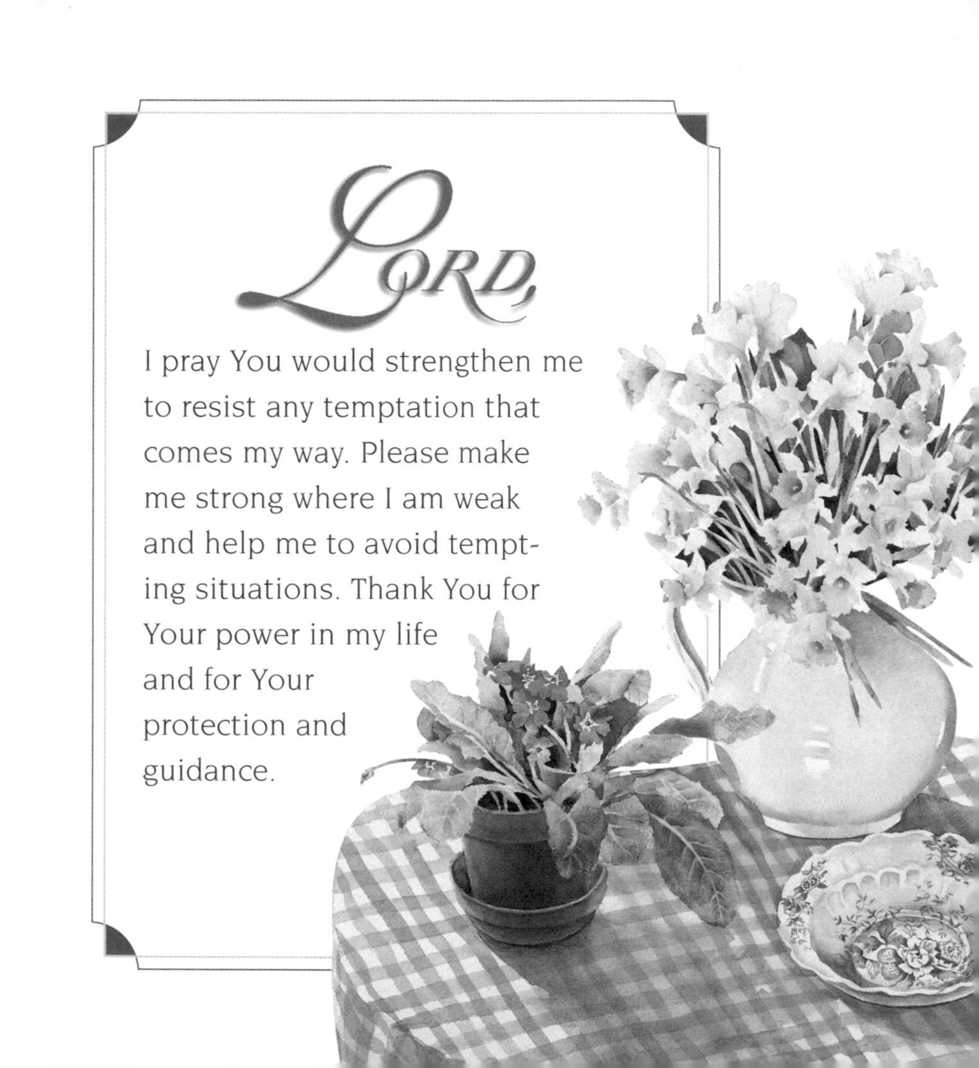

Lord,

I pray You would strengthen me to resist any temptation that comes my way. Please make me strong where I am weak and help me to avoid tempting situations. Thank You for Your power in my life and for Your protection and guidance.

Finally, brothers,
whatever is true,
whatever is noble,
whatever is right,
whatever is pure,
whatever is lovely,
whatever is admirable
—if anything
is excellent or
praiseworthy—
think about
such things.

PHILIPPIANS 4:8

NIV

I pray for protection for my mind. Please shield me from the lies of the enemy. I want so much to clearly discern between Your voice and any other. Help me to thirst for Your Word and hunger for Your truth so that I can quickly recognize wrong thinking.

To possess a Spirit-indwelt mind is the Christian's privilege under grace.

A.W. TOZER

perfect me in Your love so that fear finds no place in me. May Your love penetrate every fiber of my being, convincing me that Your love for me is greater than anything I face and that nothing can separate me from it.

I know not the way He leads me, but well do I know my Guide. What have I to fear?

MARTIN LUTHER

As God has distributed to each one, as the Lord has called each one, so let him walk.

1 CORINTHIANS 7:17

lift my eyes above the circumstances of the moment so I can see the purpose for which You created me. Help me to clearly hear Your call on my life and realize who I am in Christ.

Man, made in the image of God, has a purpose—to be in relationship to God.

FRANCIS A. SCHAEFFER

give me wisdom for every decision I make. Give me discernment to make choices based on Your revelation. I pray that You would send me godly counselors and that I would always have a teachable heart.

In darkness there is no choice. It is light that enables us to see the differences between things; and it is Christ who gives light.

A.W. HARE

A wise man will hear and increase learning, and a man of understanding will attain wise counsel.

PROVERBS 1:5

The Lord is my light and my salvation; whom shall I fear? The Lord is the strength of my life; of whom shall I be afraid?

PSALM 27:1

I will heal them and reveal to them the abundance of peace and truth.

JEREMIAH 33:6

When praying for healing, ask great things of God and expect great things from God.

ARLO F. NEWELL

I pray for Your healing touch on my life. Please make every part of my body function as it is designed to, and wherever there is anything out of balance, set it in perfect working order. Help me remember that there is a time for healing, and even when I pray and don't have immediate results, I can always trust You, my Maker.

I pray that You would protect me from accidents, diseases, dangers, and evil influences. Please keep me safe. Hide me in the shadow of Your wings.

To flee unto God is the only stay which can support us in our afflictions, the only armor which renders us invisible.

JOHN CALVIN

Gwendolyn Babbitt
©1991

The Lord is my rock and my fortress and my deliverer; my God, my strength, in whom I will trust; my shield and the horn of my salvation, my stronghold. I will call upon the Lord, who is worthy to be praised; so shall I be saved from my enemies.

PSALM 18:2,3

You, who have shown me great and severe troubles, shall revive me again, and bring me up again from the depths of the earth. You shall increase my greatness, and comfort me on every side.

PSALM 71:20,21

I know I can trust You in the midst of a trial, because You measure the weight of it on my shoulders. You alone are my refuge and my strength. I come to Your throne and ask for grace and patience as I seek You for help in this time of need.

For a Christian, even the valleys are on higher ground.

D. REGINALD THOMAS

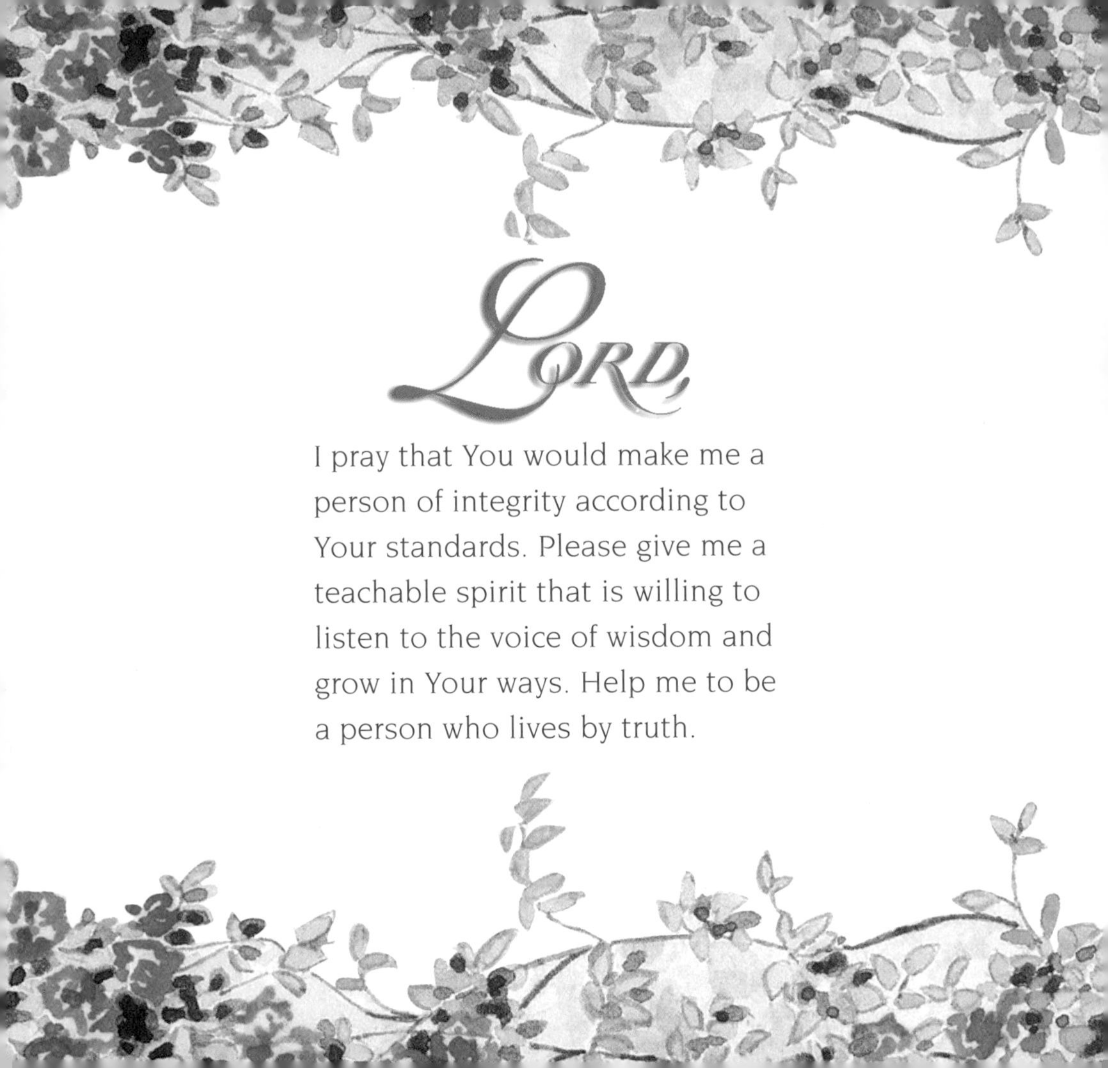

Lord,

I pray that You would make me a person of integrity according to Your standards. Please give me a teachable spirit that is willing to listen to the voice of wisdom and grow in Your ways. Help me to be a person who lives by truth.

Let integrity and uprightness preserve me, for I wait for You.

PSALM 25:21

Sleep with clean hands, either kept clean all day by integrity or washed clean at night by repentance.

JOHN DONNE

Let your light shine before men, that they may see your good deeds and praise your Father in heaven.

MATTHEW 5:16 NIV

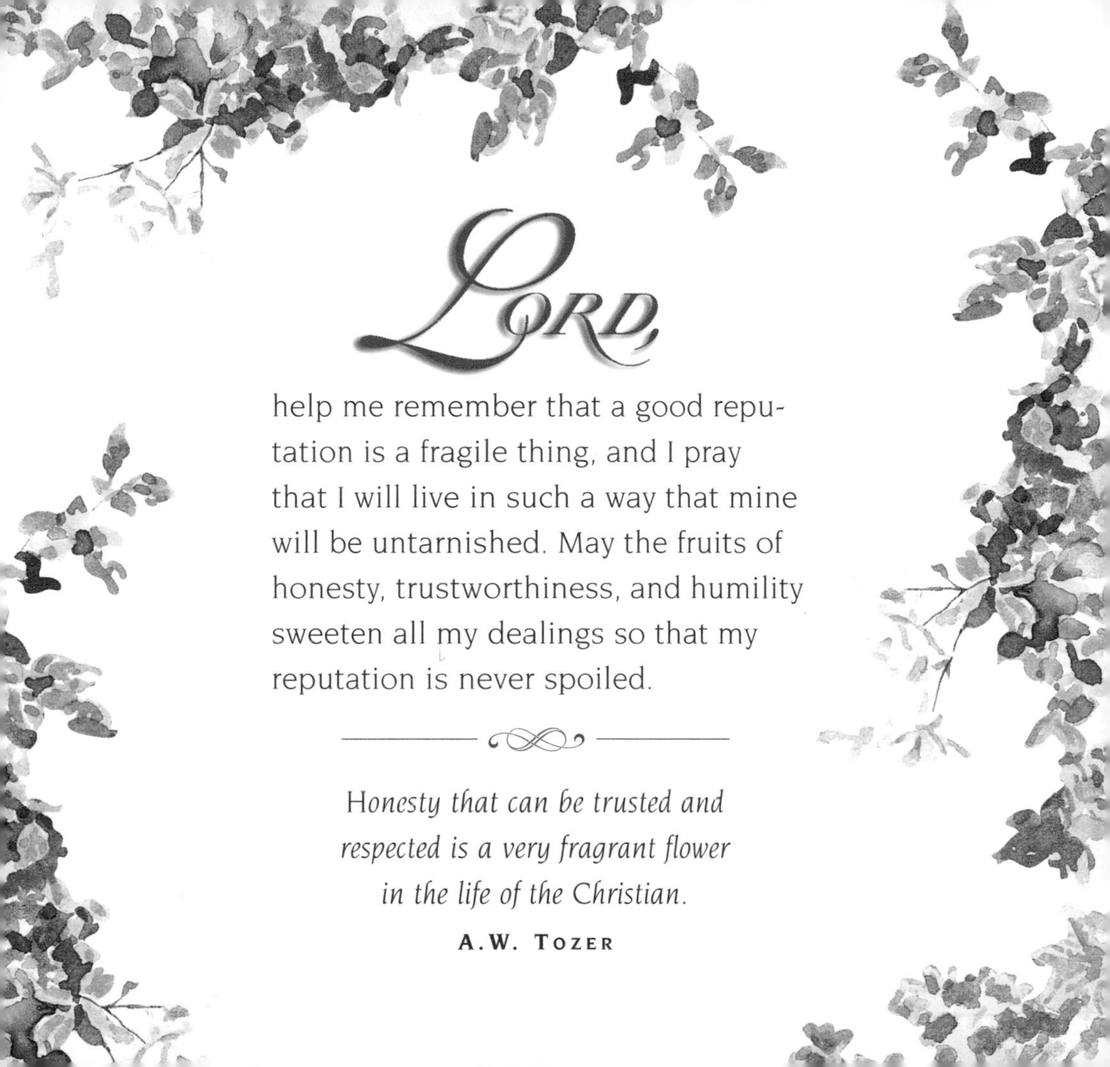

LORD,

help me remember that a good reputation is a fragile thing, and I pray that I will live in such a way that mine will be untarnished. May the fruits of honesty, trustworthiness, and humility sweeten all my dealings so that my reputation is never spoiled.

Honesty that can be trusted and respected is a very fragrant flower in the life of the Christian.

A.W. TOZER

help me set my priorities in order. Teach me how to prioritize everything so that whatever steals life away, or has no lasting purpose, will not occupy my time. I know that when I seek You first and submit my time to You, the other pieces of life fit together perfectly.

Our Father refreshes us on the journey with some pleasant inns, but will not encourage us to mistake them for home.

C.S. LEWIS

There is a time for everything, and a season for every activity under heaven.

ECCLESIASTES 3:1 NIV

Ointment and perfume delight the heart, and the sweetness of a man's friend gives delight by hearty counsel.

PROVERBS 27:9

I pray that I might have good, godly friends with whom I can openly share my heart. May they be people of wisdom who will speak truth into my life and not just what I want to hear. Help me to be just the right kind of friend in return.

Nothing is more stimulating than friends who speak truth in love.

Os Guiness

help me to hunger in my heart to really know You. Draw me close so that I may spend time in Your presence and become more like You. As I model my life before others, may it be one of complete, joyful surrender to Your perfect will.

Hasten unto Him who calls you
in the silences of your heart.

THOMAS KELLY

You will seek
Me and find Me,
when you search
for Me with all
your heart.

JEREMIAH
29:13

Do not remember the former things, nor consider the things of old. Behold, I do a new thing, now it shall spring forth; shall you not know it? I will even make a road in the wilderness and rivers in the desert.

ISAIAH 43:18,19

The past is a guidepost, not a hitching post.

L. THOMAS HOLDCROFT

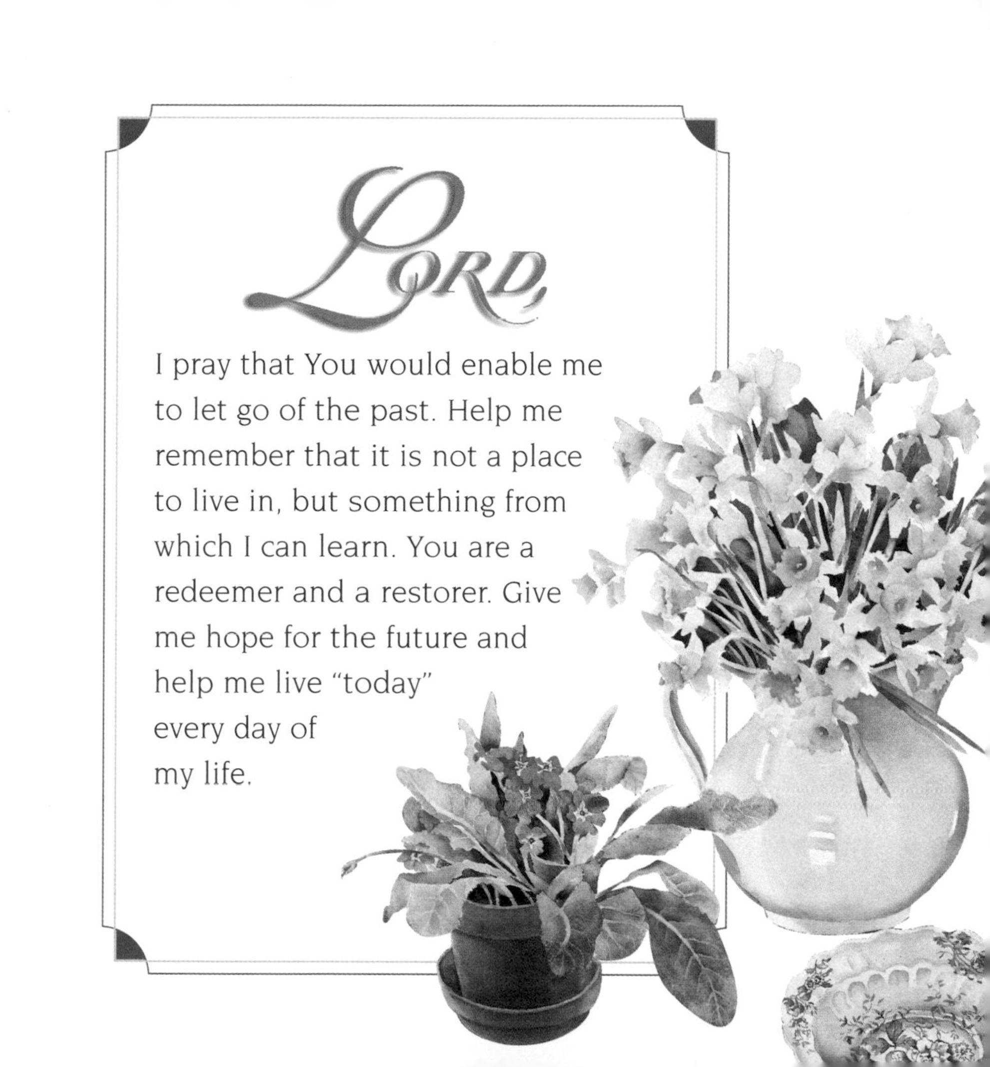

Lord,

I pray that You would enable me to let go of the past. Help me remember that it is not a place to live in, but something from which I can learn. You are a redeemer and a restorer. Give me hope for the future and help me live "today" every day of my life.

Lord,

sometimes I need help with my attitude. Release me from anger, unrest, anxiety, concerns, inner turmoil, strife, and pressure. May I not be broken in spirit because of sorrow. Instead, fill me every day with joy and peace, and help my countenance to reflect faith in Your love and care for me.

Just as the same sun melts wax and hardens clay, so Christ's presence either softens or hardens our hearts, depending on our attitude.

Rodrigo Tano

...I have learned to be content whatever the circumstances.

PHILIPPIANS 4:11 NIV

I pray that You would redeem my soul from negative emotions. Deliver me from anger, depression, anxiety, hopelessness, and fear. Thank You for the gift of laughter and songs that declare Your great faithfulness.

Those who bring sunshine to the lives of others cannot keep it from themselves.

JAMES M. BARRIE

Lord,

help me to put a guard over my tongue, and to be careful of how I speak. Fill my heart with Your love so that out of the overflow will come words that build up and not tear down.

A cup brimful of sweet water cannot spill even one drop of bitter water however suddenly jolted.

AMY CARMICHAEL

May the words of my mouth and the meditation of my heart be acceptable in Your sight, O Lord, my Strength and my Redeemer.

PSALM 19:14

I desire to have a repentant heart. Take away the pride that would cause me to deny my faults and work in my soul true humility. Thank You for Your mercies that are new every morning and the forgiveness that is so generously poured out on me.

If sin and thy heart be two,
then Christ and thy heart are one.

THOMAS BROOKS

Search me, O God, and know my heart;
try me, and know my anxieties; and see
if there is any wicked way in me, and
lead me in the way everlasting.

PSALM 139:23,24

He has put a new song in my mouth,
a hymn of praise to our God.

PSALM 40:3 NIV

because there are all kinds of things that want to put me in bondage, I pray that You would be my deliverer. I know there is no reason to feel hopeless, for You can change anything. Thank You for watching out for me and saving me.

Salvation is a happy security
and a secure happiness.

WILLIAM JENKYN

Because he has set
his love upon Me,
therefore I will
deliver him; I will
set him on high,
because he has
known My name.

PSALM 91:14

Obey My voice, and I will be your God, and you shall be My people. And walk in all the ways I have commanded you, that it may be well with you.

JEREMIAH 7:23

We all, with unveiled face, beholding as in a mirror the glory of the Lord, are being transformed into the same image from glory to glory, just as by the Spirit of the Lord.

2 CORINTHIANS 3:18

Lord,

I ask You to give me a desire to live in obedience to Your laws and Your ways. Give me a heart that longs to do Your will. May I always enjoy the peace that comes from living in total obedience to Your commands.

Only in obedience can we discover the great joy of the will of God.

SINCLAIR FERGUSON

207

I know my identity is found only in You. Quiet voices that speak of unworthiness and help me to see myself as You see me. I rejoice in freedom from self-focus and self-consciousness as I rest in You.

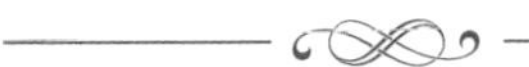

I can face myself now—because I have turned myself over to God.

LEIGHTON FORD

For you are a holy people to the
Lord your God; the Lord your God
has chosen you to be a people for Himself,
a special treasure above all the peoples
on the face of the earth.

DEUTERONOMY 7:6

thank You for loving and accepting me. You proved Your love on the cross and Your acceptance by filling me with Your Spirit. Thank You for welcoming me into Your presence, for inviting me to Your throne of grace. Help me love and accept the people You have placed in my life.

The serene beauty of a holy life
is the most powerful influence in the
world next to the power of God.

BLAISE PASCAL

I pray that You will give me an added measure of faith today. Enlarge my ability to believe in You, Your Word, Your promises, Your ways, and Your power. Thank You for opportunities to trust in You.

Faith, like a muscle, grows by stretching.

A.W. TOZER

Gwendolyn
Babbitt
©1990

I lift up to You my family relationships. Protect and preserve them from any misunderstanding or miscommunication. Grant us an abundance of compassion and forgiveness for each other and help us to value our God-ordained ties all the days of our lives.

Family life is a school for character.

Martin Luther

keep close to my heart a cherishing of others and a willingness to die to self. Help me to put others' needs before my own, and to respect and submit graciously to those in authority You have placed in my life.

Humble yourselves in the sight of the Lord, and He will lift you up.

JAMES 4:10

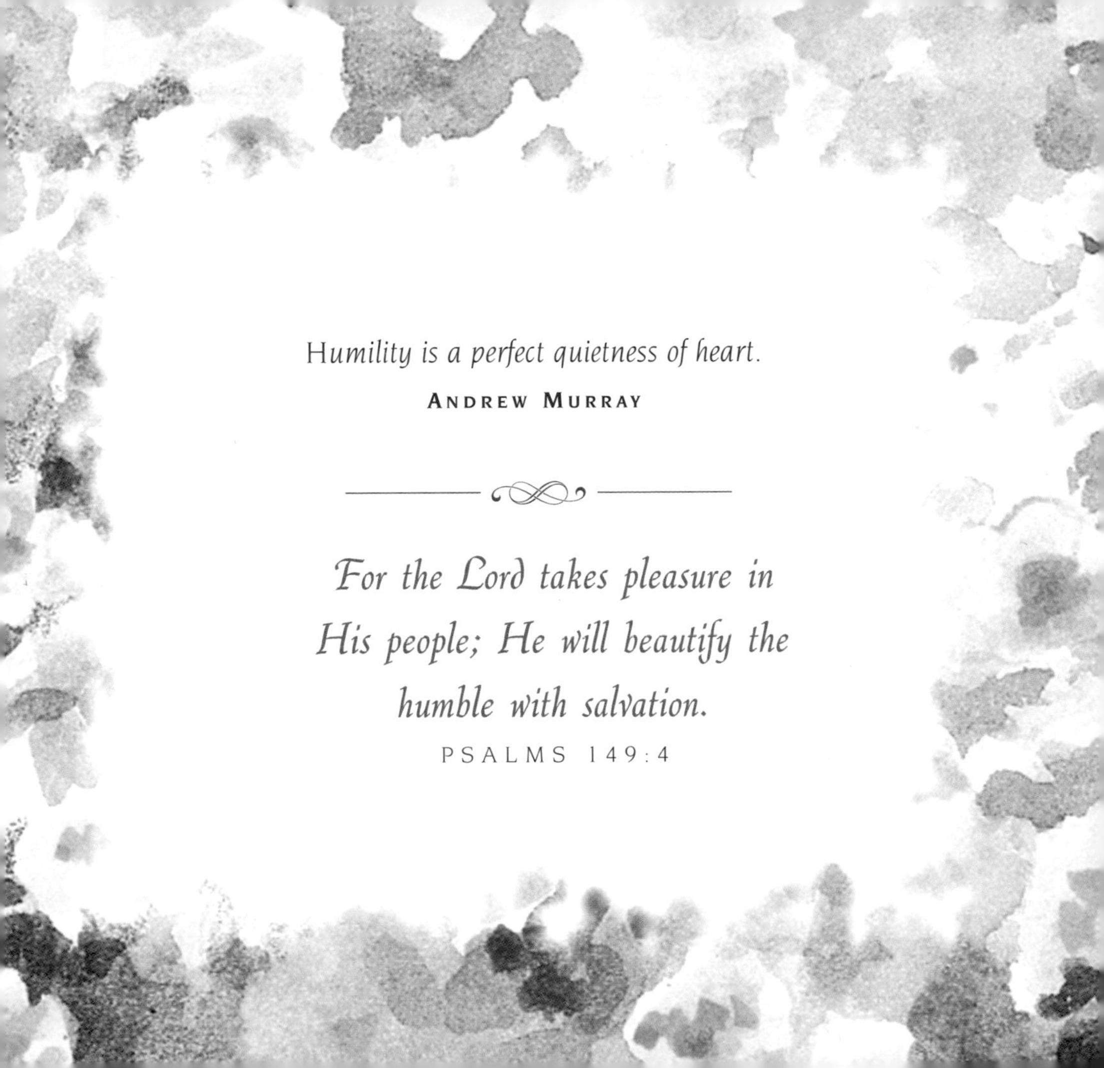

Humility is a perfect quietness of heart.

Andrew Murray

For the Lord takes pleasure in His people; He will beautify the humble with salvation.

PSALMS 149:4

please remind me how important it is to daily invite Your presence into my life and circumstances. Prayer also releases Your power in the lives of those I lift up to You. I know it pleases You when I seek You. Thank You for the welcome I know I have whenever I reach out to You.

Pour out your heart like water before the face of the Lord.

LAMENTATIONS 2:19

For I know the thoughts that I think toward you, says the Lord,
thoughts of peace and not of evil, to give you a future and a hope.

JEREMIAH 29:11

I want to find my future in You because I know You have good plans for me. I do not choose to walk in doubt and fear of what may happen, but will trust my life and future to the faithful leading of the Holy Spirit.

Every experience God gives us, every person He puts in our lives, is the perfect preparation for the future that only He can see.

CORRIE TEN BOOM